Cello Exam Pieces

ABRSM Grade 2

Selected from the syllabus from 2024

Name

Date of exam

Contents

page

Cello consultant: Alison Moncrieff-Kelly
Footnotes: Philippa Bunting

This book includes audio recordings and accompaniment tracks.
To download, please visit shop.abrsm.org/audioredeem and enter the code printed on the inside back cover.

The pieces listed above are just a selection of those on the syllabus that you can choose for your exam; the other options are listed on page 12.

Whether you are taking an ABRSM Practical or Performance Grade, pieces are at the heart of your exam; after all, playing an instrument is all about exploring, performing, and learning through repertoire.

While this book contains nine pieces in a range of styles, the full syllabus has a wealth of other exciting repertoire that we encourage you to explore – to find pieces that really inspire you, that you connect with musically and will enjoy learning, and that will allow you to perform to your very best. The full syllabus also includes duets, to give you another musical option. You can pick a mixture of pieces from this book and the wider lists if you like – you just need to have one piece from each list, A, B and C.

If you are taking a **Performance Grade**, you also need to prepare a fourth piece which is entirely your own choice. Here you have even more freedom to choose music that really speaks to you, that you want to communicate to others, and that successfully completes your programme. It can be from the syllabus lists, or somewhere else entirely. Just be sure to check the 'Selecting Repertoire' section of the Performance Grades syllabus for important requirements and options for the own-choice piece (like standard and minimum length) and the programme of four pieces overall. Finally, you need to decide what order to play your pieces in and how you, the performer, will take your audience from the very first to the very last note, including moving from one piece to another, so that the performance forms a complete musical journey.

The separate syllabuses are available at **www.abrsm.org**. Whether taking a Practical or Performance Grade, enjoy exploring the possibilities on offer!

First published in 2023 by ABRSM (Publishing) Ltd, a wholly owned subsidiary of ABRSM, 4 London Wall Place, London EC2Y 5AU, United Kingdom
© 2023 by The Associated Board of the Royal Schools of Music
Distributed worldwide by Oxford University Press

Unauthorised photocopying is illegal
All rights reserved. No part of this publication may be reproduced, recorded or transmitted in any form or by any means without the prior permission of the copyright owner.

Music origination by Julia Bovee
Cover by Kate Benjamin, James Pike & Andy Potts, with thanks to Sutton Music Service
Printed in England by Halstan & Co. Ltd, Amersham, Bucks., on materials from sustainable sources. P15883

As it has just completed its course

A:1

Da eben seinen Lauf vollbracht

from *12 Lieder auf ihrer Reise in Musik gesetzt*

Arranged by Tim Wells

Maria Theresia Paradis
(1759–1824)

Maria Theresia Paradis was a pianist, singer and composer known to the composers Salieri, Haydn and Mozart. Having lost her sight at a young age, she went on, alongside her musical studies, to invent a method for reading and writing by touch, and inspired the foundation of the Institute for Blind Youth in Paris – the first institution of its kind. Paradis' extraordinary life is celebrated in the 2022 chamber opera *The Paradis Files*, composed by Errollyn Wallen. In English, the first two lines of the song mean: 'When the most beautiful spring day has just completed its course'.

Italian Rant

Arranged by Catherine Black and Paul Harris

Anon.

This arrangement of an Italian Rant from 1663 is in a minor key but has all the energy of music meant to be danced to. A rant is a lively country dance, and the musician would typically repeat the first section with increasing exuberance and flourishes, often accompanied by a lute and a simple drum pattern. Keep bow strokes light and short to match the joyous freedom of the dance.

Adapted from *Time Pieces for Cello*, Volume 1, arranged by Catherine Black and Paul Harris (ABRSM)

The Minstrel Boy

Arranged by David Blackwell

Trad. Irish

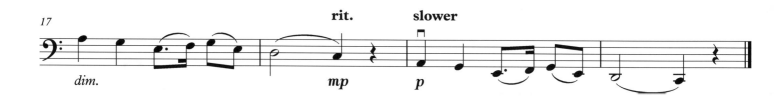

As well as music to dance to, traditional music also includes music to listen to, which is where this haunting air has its origins. The song behind it is one of leaving and loss, hence the indication to play it tenderly.

Hallelujah

B:1

Arranged by Nikki Iles

Words and music by Leonard Cohen
(1934–2016)

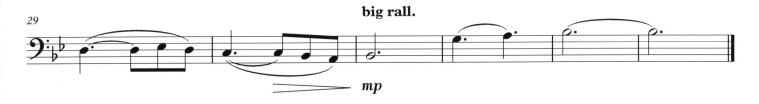

This haunting song by Canadian singer-songwriter Leonard Cohen has become very well known globally. However, after its release in 1984, it took several years before the song achieved success in covers by other artists. It came back to prominence after being used in the 2001 film *Shrek* and many artists produced their own versions, including Alexandra Burke's 2008 X Factor-winning rendition. The song is often chosen for weddings and funerals and has been described as both 'a contemporary prayer' and 'a manual for modern survival.'

B:2

Serenade

Marie Dare
(1902–76)

With its origins in Medieval Europe, the serenade is essentially a musical performance designed to celebrate or appreciate someone else. The Scottish composer Marie Dare studied at the Guildhall School of Music in London and became well known as a cello soloist. Much of her music existed only in handwritten manuscript when she died, but more and more is being discovered and published. This Serenade is written by a cellist for cellists and is a clear invitation to make your best legato sound.

Cello Exam Pieces

ABRSM Grade 2

Selected from the syllabus from 2024

Piano accompaniment

Contents

Cello consultant: Alison Moncrieff-Kelly
Footnotes: Philippa Bunting

Editorial guidance

We have taken the pieces in this book from a variety of sources. Where appropriate, we have edited the pieces to help you prepare for your performance. We have added metronome markings (in square brackets) and ornament realisations. The fingering and bowing indications have been amended where necessary to ensure a consistent approach within the album. Details of other changes or suggestions are given in the footnotes. Fingering, bowing and editorial additions are for guidance only: you do not have to follow them in the exam.

First published in 2023 by ABRSM (Publishing) Ltd,
a wholly owned subsidiary of ABRSM, 4 London Wall Place,
London EC2Y 5AU, United Kingdom
© 2023 by The Associated Board of the Royal Schools of Music
Distributed worldwide by Oxford University Press

Music origination by Julia Bovee
Cover by Kate Benjamin, James Pike & Andy Potts, with thanks to
Sutton Music Service
Printed in England by Halstan & Co. Ltd, Amersham, Bucks., on
materials from sustainable sources.

As it has just completed its course

A:1

Da eben seinen Lauf vollbracht

from *12 Lieder auf ihrer Reise in Musik gesetzt*

Arranged by Tim Wells

Maria Theresia Paradis
(1759–1824)

Maria Theresia Paradis was a pianist, singer and composer known to the composers Salieri, Haydn and Mozart. Having lost her sight at a young age, she went on, alongside her musical studies, to invent a method for reading and writing by touch, and inspired the foundation of the Institute for Blind Youth in Paris – the first institution of its kind. Paradis' extraordinary life is celebrated in the 2022 chamber opera *The Paradis Files*, composed by Errollyn Wallen. In English, the first two lines of the song mean: 'When the most beautiful spring day has just completed its course'.

A:2

Italian Rant

Arranged by Catherine Black and Paul Harris

Anon.

This arrangement of an Italian Rant from 1663 is in a minor key but has all the energy of music meant to be danced to. A rant is a lively country dance, and the musician would typically repeat the first section with increasing exuberance and flourishes, often accompanied by a lute and a simple drum pattern. Keep bow strokes light and short to match the joyous freedom of the dance.

© 1996 by The Associated Board of the Royal Schools of Music
Adapted from *Time Pieces for Cello*, Volume 1, arranged by Catherine Black and Paul Harris (ABRSM)

AB 4105

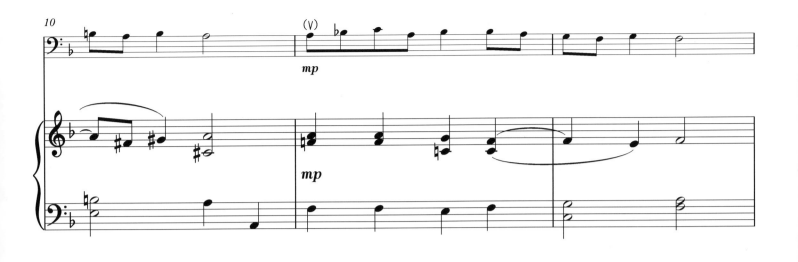

The Minstrel Boy

Arranged by David Blackwell

Trad. Irish

As well as music to dance to, traditional music also includes music to listen to, which is where this haunting air has its origins. The song behind it is one of leaving and loss, hence the indication to play it tenderly.

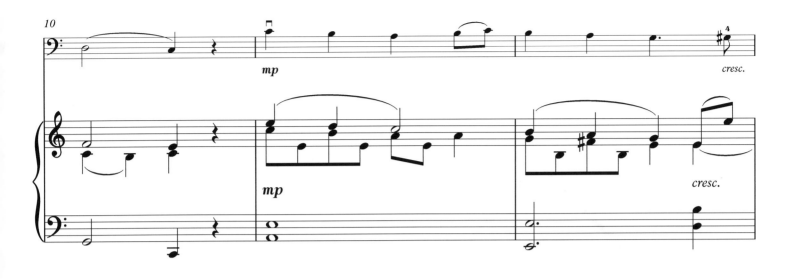

Hallelujah

B:1

Arranged by Nikki Iles

Words and music by Leonard Cohen
(1934–2016)

This haunting song by Canadian singer-songwriter Leonard Cohen has become very well known globally. However, after its release in 1984, it took several years before the song achieved success in covers by other artists. It came back to prominence after being used in the 2001 film *Shrek* and many artists produced their own versions, including Alexandra Burke's 2008 X Factor-winning rendition. The song is often chosen for weddings and funerals and has been described as both 'a contemporary prayer' and 'a manual for modern survival'.

Serenade

B:2

Marie Dare
(1902–76)

Allegretto espressivo [♩ = *c*.120]

poco rit.   a tempo

With its origins in Medieval Europe, the serenade is essentially a musical performance designed to celebrate or appreciate someone else. The Scottish composer Marie Dare studied at the Guildhall School of Music in London and became well known as a cello soloist. Much of her music existed only in handwritten manuscript when she died, but more and more is being discovered and published. This Serenade is written by a cellist for cellists and is a clear invitation to make your best legato sound.

Balmy Days

 B:3

Gerald Howard
and John York

A balmy day is one that stays pleasantly warm even when the sun goes down – a day for relaxing and doing your favourite things. This piece is about the good times, whatever those mean to you, so smile through your instrument as you fly up to fourth position, keep your bow moving at a steady speed and let happiness radiate out in your sound.

© Copyright 1998 by Guildhall School of Music & Drama

Funny Song

Thomas Hewitt Jones
(born 1984)

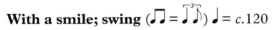

Thomas Hewitt Jones is a composer of contemporary classical and commercial music. Since winning the 2003 BBC Young Composer competition, his music has been published by many of the major music publishers and is frequently heard in concert and on radio, TV and in the cinema. Thomas says: 'I wrote, sang and performed "Funny Song" as a bit of fun in 2017. When Cavendish Music were asking for tracks for a production music album called *Vintage Oddities*, it seemed to fit perfectly. After a slow start it went megaviral on the internet and has recently become one of the most recognised pieces of music in the world, with over 10 billion streams on the TikTok platform! The original song is in A major, and I have transposed this version to C to make a fun cello piece!'

AB 4105

Paragon Rag

Arranged by David Blackwell

Scott Joplin
(1867/8–1917)

The American composer Scott Joplin was known as the 'King of Ragtime'. His most famous compositions were the rags for piano, and this is an arrangement of one of those. With its beginnings in the African American community, ragtime became a craze in the dance halls of early 20th-century America and then other parts of the world. The music's syncopated rhythms shaped the kinds of dance steps people used to dance to it, and will also influence the way you use your bow as you play across and around the beat.

C:3

Melted Mouse & Roasted Rat in Choc'late Sauce

from Wizard's Potion

Caroline Lumsden
and Ben Attwood

* slap = slap side of instrument

In the exam, the 'slap' and 'Tsss!' are optional. For the 'slap', you could (gently) tap your cello or knee, and the 'Tsss!' is like the hiss of a snake.

Caroline Lumsden trained as a violinist and singer at the Guildhall School of Music & Drama in London and then as a primary school teacher. A hallmark of her style is the humorous and imaginative approach she takes to her piece titles. This piece comes from a collection called *Wizard's Potion*, a collaboration with pianist Ben Attwood. It's up to you to decide what this particular spell conjures!

© Copyright 2003 by Peters Edition Limited, London
Reproduced by permission of Peters Edition Limited, London.

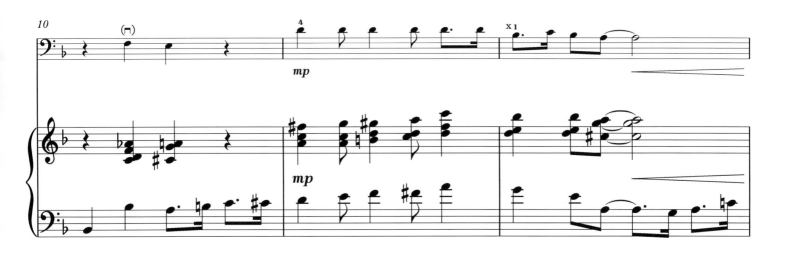

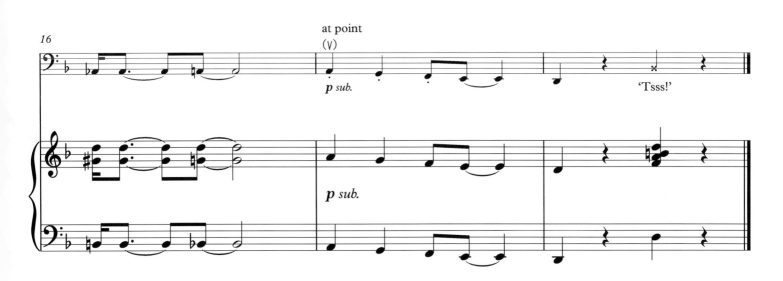

Balmy Days

Gerald Howard
and John York

A balmy day is one that stays pleasantly warm even when the sun goes down – a day for relaxing and doing your favourite things. This piece is about the good times, whatever those mean to you, so smile through your instrument as you fly up to fourth position, keep your bow moving at a steady speed and let happiness radiate out in your sound.

Funny Song

Thomas Hewitt Jones
(born 1984)

Thomas Hewitt Jones is a composer of contemporary classical and commercial music. Since winning the 2003 BBC Young Composer competition, his music has been published by many of the major music publishers and is frequently heard in concert and on radio, TV and in the cinema. Thomas says: 'I wrote, sang and performed "Funny Song" as a bit of fun in 2017. When Cavendish Music were asking for tracks for a production music album called *Vintage Oddities*, it seemed to fit perfectly. After a slow start it went megaviral on the internet and has recently become one of the most recognised pieces of music in the world, with over 10 billion streams on the TikTok platform! The original song is in A major, and I have transposed this version to C to make a fun cello piece!'

Paragon Rag

C:2

Arranged by David Blackwell

Scott Joplin
(1867/8–1917)

The American composer Scott Joplin was known as the 'King of Ragtime'. His most famous compositions were the rags for piano, and this is an arrangement of one of those. With its beginnings in the African American community, ragtime became a craze in the dance halls of early 20th-century America and then other parts of the world. The music's syncopated rhythms shaped the kinds of dance steps people used to dance to it, and will also influence the way you use your bow as you play across and around the beat.

C:3

Melted Mouse & Roasted Rat in Choc'late Sauce

from *Wizard's Potion*

Caroline Lumsden
and Ben Attwood

* slap = slap side of instrument

In the exam, the 'slap' and 'Tsss!' are optional. For the 'slap', you could (gently) tap your cello or knee, and the 'Tsss!' is like the hiss of a snake.

Caroline Lumsden trained as a violinist and singer at the Guildhall School of Music & Drama in London and then as a primary school teacher. A hallmark of her style is the humorous and imaginative approach she takes to her piece titles. This piece comes from a collection called *Wizard's Potion*, a collaboration with pianist Ben Attwood. It's up to you to decide what this particular spell conjures!

Cello Exams
from 2024

Other pieces for Grade 2

		Composer	Piece	Publication
A	4	Anon.	Hornpipe, arr. Lengyel & Pejtsik	Violoncello Music for Beginners, Vol. 1 (EMB Zeneműkiadó)
	5	J. S. Bach	Air (from *Mer hahn en neue Oberkeet*, 'Peasant Cantata', BWV 212), arr. Bruce & Wells	More Time Pieces for Cello, Vol. 1 (ABRSM)
	6	Trad. Finnish	Taivas on sininen ja valkoinen (The Sky is Blue and White), arr. Bruce & Wells	More Time Pieces for Cello, Vol. 1 (ABRSM)
	7	J. S. Bach	Minuet No. 2, arr. Suzuki & Mooney DUET/PIANO	Suzuki Cello School, Vol. 1 (Alfred) ⊕
	8	Handel	Gavotte, arr. Erhart-Schwertmann *DC to b. 8* DUET	First Duet Album for Two Cellos (Doblinger)
	9	Haydn	Minuet and Trio, arr. Nelson *without DC*	Piece by Piece 1 for Cello (Boosey & Hawkes)
	10	Haydn	Finale: Scherzo, arr. Pejtsik DUET	Violoncello Duets, Vol. 1 (EMB Zeneműkiadó)
	11	Handel	Hallelujah (from *Messiah*), arr. East	Play Baroque! (Stainer & Bell)
	12	Laubach	Soldier's March, arr. Sassmannshaus DUET	Cello Recital Album, Vol. 1 (Bärenreiter)
	13	Szokolay	Bagpipe Song (No. 2 from *Small Suite*), arr. Lengyel & Pejtsik	Violoncello Music for Beginners, Vol. 1 (EMB Zeneműkiadó)
B	4	Katherine & Hugh Colledge	Sweet Dreams (No.13 from *Fast Forward*)	Katherine & Hugh Colledge: Fast Forward for Cello (Boosey & Hawkes)
	5	Schlemüller	Lied (No.1 from *Six Easy Concert Pieces*, Op.12)	Cellissimo – Arietta (Schott) *or* Schlemüller: Six Easy Concert Pieces for Cello, Op.12 (Schott)
	6	Krogmann	The Little Prince, arr. Sassmannshaus DUET/PIANO	Cello Recital Album, Vol. 1 (Bärenreiter)
	7	Mancini & Mercer	Moon River, arr. Davies	Short Cello Pieces (Bosworth)
	8	Alan Menken & Ashman	Beauty & the Beast, arr. Davies	Short Cello Pieces (Bosworth)
	9	Trad.	Greensleeves, arr. Nelson DUET	Tunes You Know 1 for Cello Duet (Boosey & Hawkes)
	10	Dvořák	Slavonic Dance, Op. 46 No. 8, arr. Bruce & Wells	More Time Pieces for Cello, Vol. 1 (ABRSM)
	11	Thomas Gregory	An Arabian Night	Vamoosh Cello, Book 2 (Vamoosh) ⊕
	12	Ailbhe McDonagh	Shifting Sands (No.10 from *It's a Cello Thing, Book 1*)	Ailbhe McDonagh: It's a Cello Thing, Book 1 (Boosey & Hawkes)
	13	Beethoven	Irish Song, arr. Cole	Beethoven: Irish Song for Cello (Novello)
C	4	Anon. American	Hi! Says the Blackbird, arr. Waterfield & Beach	O Shenandoah! for Cello (Faber)
	5	Arlen & Harburg	We're off to see the wizard (from *The Wizard of Oz*), arr. Passchier, Hussey & Sebba DUET/PIANO	Abracadabra Cello (Third Edition) (Collins Music) ⊕
	6	Kathy & David Blackwell	Mexican Fiesta DUET/PIANO	Cello Time Runners (OUP) ⊕
	7	Mary Cohen	Hoe Down (No. 7 from *Dance Duets*) DUET	Mary Cohen: Dance Duets for Cello (Faber)
	8	Katherine & Hugh Colledge	The Ceilidh (No. 21 from *Fast Forward*)	Katherine & Hugh Colledge: Fast Forward for Cello (Boosey & Hawkes)
	9	Thomas Gregory	Smooth Operator	Vamoosh Cello, Book 2 (Vamoosh) ⊕
	10	Tim Wells	Happy Places	More Time Pieces for Cello, Vol. 1 (ABRSM)
	11	Kathy & David Blackwell	Paris Café DUET/PIANO	Cello Time Runners (OUP) ⊕
	12	Joanna Borrett	Lindy Hop Rock (No. 2 from *Inspiration Cello! Book 1*) DUET	Joanna Borrett: Inspiration Cello! Book 1 (United Music Publishing)
	13	Ailbhe McDonagh	Pasta Dance (No.14 from *It's a Cello Thing, Book 1*)	Ailbhe McDonagh: It's a Cello Thing, Book 1 (Boosey & Hawkes)

⊕ Accompaniment(s) published separately, see www.abrsm.org/syllabusclarifications